Living as a Confident Daughter of God

A Faith-Sharing Guide for Catholic Women

Living as a Confident Daughter of God

A Faith-Sharing Guide for Catholic Women

Patricia Mitchell

The Word Among Us Press
9639 Doctor Perry Road
Ijamsville, Maryland 21754
www.wordamongus.org

12 11 10 09 08 1 2 3 4 5
ISBN: 978-1-59325-112-3

Unless otherwise noted, Scripture passages contained herein are from the New Revised Standard Version Bible: Catholic Edition, copyright © 1989, 1993 Division of Christian Education of the National Council of the Churches of Christ in the United States of America. All rights reserved. Used with permission.

Excerpts from the English translation of the *Catechism of the Catholic Church* for use in the United States of America, copyright © 1994, United States Catholic Conference, Inc.—Libreria Editrice Vaticana. Used with permission.

Nihil Obstat: The Reverend Michael Morgan, Chancellor
Censor Librorum
October 15, 2007
Imprimatur: +Most Reverend Victor Galeone
Bishop of Saint Augustine
October 15, 2007

Cover design by David Crosson

Made and printed in the United States of America

Library of Congress Cataloging-in-Publication Data

Mitchell, Patricia, 1953-
Living as a confident daughter of God : a faith-sharing guide for Catholic women / Patricia Mitchell.
p. cm.
ISBN 978-1-59325-112-3 (alk. paper)
1. Catholic women--Religious life. 2. Confidence--Religious aspects--Christianity. I. Title.
BX2353.M583 2008
248.8'43088282--dc22

2007040532

Contents

Acknowledgments

I am grateful to Angela Burrin, Jeanne Kun, and Theresa Difato, who took the time to review the manuscript and who offered incredibly helpful and wise comments. Thanks to everyone on The Word Among Us Press team who contributed to the publication of this book, including Jeff Smith, Don Cooper, Bert Ghezzi, Margaret Procario, David Crosson, Diane Menapace, Carrie Smoot, and Ginger Roché. I especially want to thank my husband, John, for his constant encouragement, support, and steadfast love (and for sending me to my office when I didn't feel like writing). I am also indebted to my "sisters in the Lord" for showing me, on a daily basis, what it means to be a beloved and confident daughter of God.

Introduction

For we have become partners of Christ, if only we hold
our first confidence firm to the end.
—Hebrews 3:14

What image comes into your mind when you think of a confident woman? Perhaps you think of someone who knows who she is and what she does well. Perhaps she exudes an air of self-assurance. Her confidence in herself allows others to place their confidence in her as well. Confidence is a quality that most people want to have, which is why there are plenty of self-help books available on the topic—especially for women.

This faith-sharing guide, *Living as a Confident Daughter of God*, is about growing in confidence, too—but not in yourself. Instead, it's about growing in confidence of God, of his promises and his call in your life. We have confidence in God when we know who he is and what he wants for us. We can place our trust in all that he wants to do—in us, for us, and for his people. We do gain self-confidence as a result of the confidence we place in the Lord, but it is confidence based not on our limited human resources but on the amazing reality that God, through Christ, has made us part of his family. We are his daughters, "partners of Christ," and we share in the divine life of the Trinity. What greater confidence booster could we desire!

Living as a Confident Daughter of God was written after the enthusiastic reception of a similar guide, *Living as a Beloved Daughter of God*. The aim of both guides is to help women grow in their relationships with God and with one another. Bible studies and faith-sharing guides help us build both of these crucial relationships. Through them, we take time out of our busy lives to sit down with the Lord as we reflect on the truths of Scripture and the church.

And when we share what we have learned with other women, we not only benefit from their insights, but we also get to know them in a deeper way. How pleasing this must be to our Lord, who calls us into relationship with him as our Father and with other women as our sisters in Christ.

This faith-sharing guide is divided into two parts. The first eight sessions are designed to help us recall and internalize God's promises—among them his promise to love us unconditionally, to be with us at all times, to give us grace, and to hear our prayers. As we reflect on God's promises, we become more confident that he is a God who fulfills those promises.

The second eight sessions help us gain confidence in God's call in our lives. God calls us to be newly created in him, to be holy women who understand our feminine gifts and our vocation, who use our talents and gifts, who work for justice, and who spread his word. We have been given a great call, and we can answer that call, confident that Jesus will be at our side at all times.

Each of the sixteen sessions begins with an introduction and a short story about a woman who is faced with a challenge that requires her to exercise her faith. (Some are based on true stories.) A Scripture passage and excerpts from the *Catechism of the Catholic Church* and other church documents have been selected to support the theme for that session. The questions provide a basis for personal reflection and group discussion.

Guidelines for Small Group Meetings

A strong facilitator is of great value in using this guide. She doesn't need to be an expert in Scripture or church doctrine, although a knowledge of both would be helpful. And she doesn't function as a teacher. Rather, she "guides" the group, by keeping everyone focused on the subject, seeing that each woman in the group has an opportunity to participate, and keeping the discussion moving along.

If the group is newly organized, we suggest that one person serve as facilitator. After the group has bonded and the women have become comfortable with one another, the facilitator's role may be rotated among the women who are interested in leading the discussion. This will prepare women to lead another group when the current one grows beyond eight or ten members.

Here are some guidelines that will help the members of your group get the most out of their time together. You can download a more detailed chapter-by-chapter facilitator's guide for this book by logging on to www.wordamongus.org/confident_daughter.

Opening Prayer

A time of prayer to open your sessions will provide everyone with the opportunity to come into the presence of the Lord. The specific format is up to you. You may choose to begin with a traditional prayer, such as the Our Father or the Hail Mary, or even a decade of the rosary. Or, you can try spontaneous prayer from the group or a brief prayer service planned by one of the participants. You may also want to sing a hymn or play a CD.

Accountability

Preparing ahead for the sessions will ensure greater participation and more fruitful discussions. So it's important that all the women plan to devote some time before each meeting to reading the Scripture passages and selections from the church documents and answering the questions that follow. Scripture texts from the New Revised Standard Version are included in each chapter so that the members of the group can all refer to the same translation. Short selections from the *Catechism* and other church documents are reprinted in this guide, but participants can read more on the topic by going to those sources directly. The complete *Catechism*, as well as most church documents, are readily available online.

Facilitators should encourage participants to attend as many meetings as possible. Not only does regular participation provide coherence and consistency to the group's discussions, it also demonstrates that members value one another and are committed to sharing their lives with one another.

Confidentiality

Faith sharing can only be honest and personal if participants feel that they can completely trust one another. Facilitators should stress ahead of time that whatever is said at the meetings is strictly confidential. It's a good idea to remind the group of that point periodically, as well. Then, as the women in the group become more comfortable with one another, they will feel increasingly able to share their faith experiences on ever deeper levels.

Timing

Each session is designed to be covered in ninety minutes. Depending on the interaction of the group, how well the participants have prepared, or the amount of time spent in sharing and prayer, the time needed to cover the material in each session may vary. Nevertheless, since the participants have other commitments, it's important to try to start and stop on time. You may decide to skip some of the questions so that you still end on schedule. Or, if a particularly interesting discussion is underway, the group may choose to continue that session at the next meeting. Above all, try to be sensitive to the needs of the members of your group, since they are making a time commitment in order to participate.

Concluding Prayer

The meetings should always be closed with a prayer of thanksgiving. This would be a good time to pray for any of the women in the group who have a special need.

Other Suggestions

■ Start with a few moments of socializing. You may want to offer drinks or snacks at the meeting.

■ Be flexible. While a predictable format is helpful, flexibility is also necessary at times to adjust to an individual's needs.

■ Encourage personal witnessing and testimonies to build faith.

■ Form teams of two women who will call each other during the week to encourage one another.

■ Be ready to welcome new members to the group and to break up into two groups if the original group grows too large.

■ Space the sessions according to your group's needs. If the members of your group find it too difficult to meet for sixteen weeks consecutively, they can agree to meet for eight weeks and then begin sessions nine through sixteen at a later time. Or, you can meet biweekly or monthly—whatever works for your group.

As you journey through these sixteen sessions, may you experience God's love for you as his beloved and confident daughter, and may this love inflame your heart so that you become a powerful witness to Christ and his church.

Patricia Mitchell

Part One

Confidence in God's Promises

Confidence in God's Embrace

Have you ever imagined God greeting you with a warm embrace? That's how the father in Jesus' famous parable greeted his prodigal son. For many of us, however, it can be a challenge to believe in a God who is eager and ready to meet us wherever we find ourselves.

Maybe that's because we tend to focus on our shortcomings and sins and wonder how the all-perfect God can love us just as we are. We may have experienced conditional love in our past and can't imagine that God will love us when we fail. Yet what we find hard to believe is actually true: God is head-over-heels in love with us! In fact, we delight him and give him pleasure, just because we are his daughters. If we are going to live as confident daughters of our heavenly Father, we first need to be confident in God's unconditional love and limitless mercy.

Sherry had been raised Catholic, but during her turbulent young adult years she left the church. She was glad to be back but was still ashamed of some of the things she had done during the years she had been away. She knew on an intellectual level that God had forgiven her youthful transgressions and that he loved her. Still, she was reluctant to try to get closer to him, because she had never really experienced his love in a consistent or palpable way.

When a moms' group formed at her parish, Sherry decided to join. The women often went to daily Mass after their meetings, sitting in the back pews as their young children climbed over them, and they invited her to join them. Sherry began to notice that on the days she went to Mass, she felt a sense of peace and joy for hours afterwards. One day Olivia, one of the moms in the group whom Sherry especially admired, shared about her past. Sherry was amazed at how similar it was to her own! Olivia lent Sherry some spiritual books to read and encouraged her to pray and to read the Bible each day.

As Sherry persevered in her daily prayer and spent more time with the women in the moms' group, she realized that her ideas about God had been all wrong. He wasn't a distant God who was ready to pounce on her every time she did something wrong. He was a loving and merciful God, always ready to forgive, always desiring an ever deeper and more intimate relationship with her.

Scripture: Luke 15:11-32

[11]Then Jesus said, "There was a man who had two sons. [12]The younger of them said to his father, 'Father, give me the share of the property that will belong to me.' So he divided his property between them. [13]A few days later the younger son gathered all he had and traveled to a distant country, and there he squandered his property in dissolute living. [14]When he had spent everything, a severe famine took place throughout that country, and he began to be in need. [15]So he went and hired himself out to one of the citizens of that country, who sent him to his fields to feed the pigs. [16]He would gladly have filled himself with

the pods that the pigs were eating; and no one gave him anything. ¹⁷But when he came to himself he said, 'How many of my father's hired hands have bread enough and to spare, but here I am dying of hunger! ¹⁸I will get up and go to my father, and I will say to him, "Father, I have sinned against heaven and before you; ¹⁹I am no longer worthy to be called your son; treat me like one of your hired hands."' ²⁰So he set off and went to his father. But while he was still far off, his father saw him and was filled with compassion; he ran and put his arms around him and kissed him. ²¹Then the son said to him, 'Father, I have sinned against heaven and before you; I am no longer worthy to be called your son.' ²²But the father said to his slaves, 'Quickly, bring out a robe—the best one—and put it on him; put a ring on his finger and sandals on his feet. ²³And get the fatted calf and kill it, and let us eat and celebrate; ²⁴for this son of mine was dead and is alive again; he was lost and is found!' And they began to celebrate.

²⁵"Now his elder son was in the field; and when he came and approached the house, he heard music and dancing. ²⁶He called one of the slaves and asked what was going on. ²⁷He replied, 'Your brother has come, and your father has killed the fatted calf, because he has got him back safe and sound.' ²⁸Then he became angry and refused to go in. His father came out and began to plead with him. ²⁹But he answered his father, 'Listen! For all these years I have been working like a slave for you, and I have never disobeyed your command; yet you have never given me even a young goat so that I might celebrate with my friends. ³⁰But when this son of yours came back, who has devoured your property with prostitutes, you killed the fatted calf for him!' ³¹Then the father said to him, 'Son, you are always with me, and all that is mine is yours. ³²But we had to celebrate and rejoice, because this brother of yours was dead and has come to life; he was lost and has been found.'"

1. After spending his inheritance "in dissolute living," the younger son never expected to be called a son of his father again. Why were his expectations so off base?

_____

_____

_____

_____

_____

2. How would the actions and attitudes of the older son been different if he had really known that his father loved him so deeply? What did his father do for him that he failed to perceive as acts of love?

_____

_____

_____

_____

_____

3. Was there ever a time in your life when you felt like the younger son? Like the older son? Were you able to come back to your heavenly Father and accept his love? If so, share what happened.

_____

_____

_____

_____

_____

From the Church:

The human heart is heavy and hardened. God must give man a new heart. Conversion is first of all a work of the grace of God who makes our hearts return to him. . . . God gives us the strength to begin anew. It is in discovering the greatness of God's love that our heart is shaken by the horror and weight of sin. . . . The human heart is converted by looking upon him whom our sins have pierced. (*Catechism of the Catholic Church*, 1432)

1. Have you ever experienced "the greatness of God's love," even for just a moment? What was it like? Was it a fleeting experience, or do you experience it regularly?

_____

_____

_____

_____

_____

2. How is a "heavy and hardened" heart an obstacle to accepting God's loving embrace? What steps could you take or have you taken in the past to soften your heart toward God or others?

_____

_____

_____

_____

_____

3. Why is Jesus on the cross, "whom our sins have pierced," the ultimate testament of God's love for us? Is that how you look at the cross? Why or why not?

_____

_____

_____

_____

_____

For Further Reflection and Discussion:

1. Why do you think we are sometimes tempted to believe that God loves us less because of our sinfulness? How is that a contradiction of the good news?

_____

_____

_____

_____

_____

2. Have the knowledge and experience of God's love in your own life changed the way you live? If so, how?

_____

_____

_____

_____

_____

3. How might failing to see your own self-worth prevent you from fully experiencing God's embrace? What might the Lord say to you if you told him you weren't worthy of his love and mercy?

_____

_____

_____

_____

_____

4. How does confidence in God's love make us more loving toward others? How does confidence in God's mercy make us more merciful toward others?

_____

_____

_____

_____

_____

Confidence in God's Presence

When we were baptized, Christ came to live in us. We sense his presence in the beauty of nature and in those we love. In the Eucharist, he is truly present: body, blood, soul, and divinity. In the Sacrament of Confirmation, we received the fullness of the Holy Spirit. Whether we are going about our daily routine or experiencing a crisis, we can be confident that God is with us. We can be confident of his promise that he will never leave us or forsake us (see Hebrews 13:5).

Several months before Kathy and her husband, Michael, were scheduled to move into their new retirement home, Michael suffered a stroke and was rushed to the emergency room. Kathy and her children gathered around the hospital bed, praying for Michael's recovery. However, he sank into a coma and died a week later. Numb with shock, Kathy got through the funeral with the help of family and friends. Then she was faced with building a new life without her husband of thirty-eight years.

Looking back, Kathy remembers the darkness and grief of the days and months that followed her husband's death. However, she also remembers that she often felt an overwhelming and abiding sense of God's presence in her life. This conviction only grew stronger as time went on. Kathy had been a practicing Catholic all her life. Now, she believed, the Lord was using the emptiness and loneliness of grief to call her into a deeper, more intimate relationship with him.

Scripture: Psalm 23

[1]The LORD is my shepherd, I shall not want.
  [2]He makes me lie down in green pastures;
he leads me beside still waters;
  [3]he restores my soul.
He leads me in right paths
  for his name's sake.

[4]Even though I walk through the darkest valley,
  I fear no evil;
for you are with me;
  your rod and your staff—
  they comfort me.

[5]You prepare a table before me
  in the presence of my enemies;
you anoint my head with oil;
  my cup overflows.

[6]Surely goodness and mercy shall follow me
  all the days of my life,
and I shall dwell in the house of the LORD
  my whole life long.

1. In what ways does the image of God as your shepherd help to assure you of his constant presence in your life?

_____

_____

_____

_____

_____

2. What verbs does the psalmist use to describe the ways God tends to him? What does this say about God's activity in our lives?

_____

_____

_____

_____

_____

3. The psalmist declares his intention to dwell in the house of the Lord. What positive steps do you take to stay close to the Lord each day, especially when you are feeling discouraged or abandoned? (Some possibilities: daily Mass and prayer time, adoration of the Blessed Sacrament, taking a walk to enjoy nature, or listening to inspirational music.)

_____

_____

_____

_____

_____

From the Church:

Even now we are called to be a dwelling for the Most Holy Trinity. (*Catechism*, 260)

From a Prayer of Blessed Elizabeth of the Trinity:
"Oh my God, Trinity whom I adore . . . Grant my soul peace. Make it your heaven, your beloved dwelling and the place of your rest. May I never abandon you there, but may I be there, whole and entire, completely vigilant in my faith, entirely adoring, and wholly given over to your creative action." (*Catechism*, 260)

1. How does an understanding of the truth that God dwells in our inmost souls help us when we pray? When we look to God for strength and comfort?

_____

_____

_____

_____

2. What opportunities do you have during the course of the day to turn to God to speak to him or praise him? How can this practice of being in God's presence help you grow in your relationship with him?

_____

_____

_____

_____

3. How often have you prayed like Blessed Elizabeth to invite God into your soul? What do you think would be the benefits of such a prayer?

_____

_____

_____

_____

_____

For Further Reflection and Discussion:

1. God is present to us in the sacraments and in Scripture. How does frequent celebration of the Eucharist and reconciliation help us to grow closer to Christ? What Scripture passage or story has helped you sense that God is with you?

_____

_____

_____

_____

2. Share a time in your life when you most strongly felt the Lord's presence. How did this experience affect your faith? The faith of those around you?

_____

_____

_____

_____

3. Many saints, including St. Thérèse of Lisieux and Blessed Mother Teresa, have endured a "dark night of the soul" in which they were unable to experience God's presence. How do you think they were able to stay faithful and confident of God's love under such circumstances? How can their example help us in those times when we are unable to feel God's presence?

_____

_____

_____

_____

_____

4. We often experience God's presence in other people. Name some ways we can "be Christ" to those we encounter each day.

_____

_____

_____

_____

_____

Confidence in God's Grace

God is never stingy with his grace! Through the death and resurrection of Jesus, we have all the grace we need to live a life pleasing to God. We should always be confident that God wants to give us his grace to help us live out our vocation and build his kingdom. All we have to do is ask and then stand firm in the knowledge that he will give it to us.

When Amy discovered that she was expecting a baby, she and her husband, Joe, were thrilled. They spent the months of her pregnancy fixing up a nursery and getting their home in order. Amy delivered a healthy baby girl, whom they named Jessica, and she and Joe thanked God for such a great gift.

However, when Jessica turned two, Amy and Joe started to notice some changes in her behavior. Jessica, who had once been so eager to talk, avoided eye contact and became quiet. She often turned her head away when Amy tried to kiss her. Amy and Joe discussed these and other disturbing changes with their pediatrician. After many medical visits and tests, Jessica was diagnosed with autism. Amy and Joe were crushed.

The challenges of parenting an autistic child often were overwhelming. Amy found that she had to beg God for his grace each morning just to get through the day. It was difficult just to find a few minutes to pray, but Amy made the effort, always asking for big doses of love, patience, and wisdom. There were still tough moments, but the more Amy's prayers were answered, the more confident she became that God would give her the grace she needed to be a good mother to Jessica.

Scripture: Luke 1:26-38

[26]In the sixth month the angel Gabriel was sent by God to a town in Galilee called Nazareth, [27]to a virgin engaged to a man whose name was Joseph, of the house of David. The virgin's name was Mary. [28]And he came to her and said, "Greetings, favored one! The Lord is with you." [29]But she was much perplexed by his words and pondered what sort of greeting this might be. [30]The angel said to her, "Do not be afraid, Mary, for you have found favor with God. [31]And now, you will conceive in your womb and bear a son, and you will name him Jesus. [32]He will be great, and will be called the Son of the Most High, and the Lord God will give to him the throne of his ancestor David. [33]He will reign over the house of Jacob forever, and of his kingdom there will be no end." [34]Mary said to the angel, "How can this be, since I am a virgin?" [35]The angel said to her, "The Holy Spirit will come upon you, and the power of the Most High will overshadow you; therefore the child to be born will be holy; he will be called Son of God. [36]And now, your relative Elizabeth in her old age has also conceived a son; and this is the sixth month for her who was said to be barren. [37]For nothing will be impossible with God." [38]Then Mary said, "Here am I, the servant of the Lord; let it be with me according to your word." Then the angel departed from her.

1. The angel Gabriel's news must have startled and overwhelmed Mary, and yet she was able to respond with her *fiat,* or "yes," to God. What does this say about her faith? Her confidence in God?

_____

_____

_____

_____

_____

2. What additional events in Mary's life do you think required her to ask for—and receive—God's grace?

_____

_____

_____

_____

_____

3. What character traits are necessary for us to be able to cooperate with God's grace as Mary did? How can we best develop such traits?

_____

_____

_____

_____

_____

From the Church:

Our justification comes from the grace of God. Grace is *favor*, the free and undeserved help that God gives us to respond to his call to become children of God, adoptive sons, partakers of the divine nature and of eternal life. (*Catechism*, 1996)

Grace is first and foremost the gift of the Spirit who justifies and sanctifies us. But grace also includes the gifts that the Spirit grants us to associate us with his work, to enable us to collaborate in the salvation of others and in the growth of the Body of Christ, the Church. (*Catechism*, 2003)

1. What does grace mean to you? When has grace helped you to respond to God's call and plan for your life?

_____

_____

_____

_____

_____

2. Why is it important to view grace as "free" and "undeserved"? Why are we often tempted to believe that we need to earn grace or need to be worthy to receive it?

_____

_____

_____

_____

_____

3. What is the relationship between the Holy Spirit and grace? How does the Spirit work in dispensing grace?

_____

_____

_____

_____

_____

For Further Reflection and Discussion:

1. Share about a time in your life when you clearly recognized that you got through a challenging situation or defeated a particular temptation only by the grace of God. Take the time to thank the Lord for this grace.

_____

_____

_____

_____

_____

2. Think of a situation or relationship with which you are currently struggling. What concrete action or step of faith can you take in that situation to demonstrate your confidence that God will give you the grace you need to resolve it?

_____

_____

_____

_____

_____

3. We receive grace when we celebrate the sacraments, especially when we regularly receive the Sacraments of Reconciliation and the Eucharist. Why is it important to have expectant faith that through the sacraments you will receive the grace you need to live a life pleasing to God?

_____

_____

_____

_____

_____

4. God's grace enabled Mary to fulfill her calling to be the mother of his Son, Jesus. In what specific ways can God's grace help you in the various roles you are called to fulfill as daughter, wife, mother, friend, parishioner, or employee?

_____

_____

_____

_____

Confidence in Our Freedom in Christ

4

When you hear the word "freedom," what comes to your mind? Do you think of the individual freedoms we enjoy, like freedom of speech and worship? Do you think of a young adult without ties or commitments? Do you think of people who believe they can do whatever they want? For Christians, freedom has a specific meaning. As baptized daughters of the living God, we are free because Christ's death on the cross has set us free—from sin, from bad habits, from anxiety, depression, bitterness, fear, or anything else that hinders us from drawing closer to Jesus. We need to have confidence in the freedom that Christ won for us.

For many years, Barbara had been a compulsive shopper. She often tried to fight the temptation to purchase things she didn't need and couldn't afford, and for a week or two she'd be successful. But as soon as she felt stressed or depressed, she would invariably drive to the mall and drive up the balance on her credit card. Her shopping habits put great stress not only on the family finances but also on her marriage.

When her friend Angie offered to pray with her to free her from her shopping addiction, Barbara was put off. She didn't think she had an addiction, and she didn't see how prayer would help. She only needed more willpower to stay away from the mall. But when her high credit card bills put their house in jeopardy, Barbara called her friend. Angie explained how Jesus had already set her free by his death on the cross. Willpower by itself wasn't going to help her. She needed to place her faith in the truth that she was free in Christ: she didn't have to be a slave to her out-of-control shopping habits. Prayer, Scripture reading, support from friends, and regular sessions with a Christian counselor helped Barbara believe in what Christ had done for her. In those times when she was tempted to buy something she didn't need, Barbara tried to recognize that her real needs were emotional and spiritual. She learned to turn to God and to call her husband or a friend for prayer and support.

Scripture: John 8:31-36

[31]Then Jesus said to the Jews who had believed in him, "If you continue in my word, you are truly my disciples; [32]and you will know the truth, and the truth will make you free." [33]They answered him, "We are descendants of Abraham and have never been slaves to anyone. What do you mean by saying, 'You will be made free'?"

[34]Jesus answered them, "Very truly, I tell you, everyone who commits sin is a slave to sin. [35]The slave does not have a permanent place in the household; the son has a place there forever. [36]So if the Son makes you free, you will be free indeed."

1. What kind of freedom did Jesus promise the Jewish believers? How did it differ from the freedom that they alluded to?

_____

_____

_____

_____

_____

2. What do you think Jesus meant when he told the Jews to "continue in my word"? How does that make us his disciples?

_____

_____

_____

_____

_____

3. As a permanent member of the household of God, the church (see verse 35), we have been given the Sacrament of Reconciliation, which gives us a concrete way to know that we are forgiven. When you receive absolution from the priest in this sacrament, do you feel confident that you have been freed from sin? Why or why not?

_____

_____

_____

_____

_____

From the Church:

By his glorious Cross Christ has won salvation for all men. He redeemed them from the sin that held them in bondage. "For freedom Christ has set us free" (Galatians 5:1). . . . The Holy Spirit has been given to us and, as the Apostle teaches, "Where the Spirit of the Lord is, there is freedom" (2 Corinthians 3:17). Already we glory in the "liberty of the children of God" (Romans 8:21). (*Catechism,* 1741)

1. When you look at a cross, how often do you see it as the way God has emancipated you from sin? How can greater faith in what Jesus accomplished on the cross bring victory over sin in your life?

_____

_____

_____

_____

_____

2. Why does St. Paul say that the Holy Spirit brings us freedom? How can being more attuned to the Spirit help us break free of habits and behaviors in our lives that have a negative effect on ourselves or others?

_____

_____

_____

_____

_____

3. According to the *Catechism,* our liberty as children of God should be an experience and a reality that we "glory" in. Yet how often do we feel burdened, not free! Why do you think many Christian women fail to fully experience the liberty that is theirs as daughters of God?

_____

_____

_____

_____

_____

For Further Reflection and Discussion:

1. What do you think is the difference between a secular and a Christian view of freedom? How do secular attitudes of freedom impact us as Christians? As women?

_____

_____

_____

_____

_____

2. When have you felt most free in your life? Why? What changes can you make in your life today that will bring you more freedom?

_____

_____

_____

_____

_____

3. God wants us to be free not only from sin, but also from fear, anxiety, negative thinking, and anything that leads us away from him. Name some areas of your life in which you desire more freedom. Come before the cross of Christ, and ask him to free you from whatever is burdening you.

_____

_____

_____

_____

_____

4. In your most important relationships, how free do you feel to give and receive love? What may be holding you back?

_____

_____

_____

_____

_____

Confidence in the Power of Prayer

*D*o you believe in the power of prayer? We say that we do, but deep down we often harbor doubts that our prayers are heard by God or that they will really change anything. Perhaps we have asked God for something that is close to our hearts, only to see our prayer go unanswered. Perhaps we see someone else's prayer answered and wonder why we don't see that power manifested in our own lives.

We know that our heavenly Father loves us and wants the best for us. We are called to act on that truth by having confidence that prayer is powerful. We can pray with expectant faith that God will hear us. When we don't see our prayers answered, we are called to trust—and to continue praying.

For seventeen years, St. Monica had to trust that God would give her the deepest desire of her heart—the conversion of her son, Augustine. In his *Confessions*, St. Augustine describes how he set sail for Rome without telling his mother, leaving her in anguish by the seacoast in Carthage after she realized what he had done. Monica had prayed that Augustine would not leave her. God did not intervene to prevent Augustine from leaving Carthage, but he did answer the deepest prayer of her heart: it was through the people that Augustine met in Rome and Milan that led to his conversion. In 387, Augustine was baptized by St. Ambrose, the bishop of Milan. Later that year, Monica died, at peace that the work of praying for her son's salvation was completed.

Scripture: John 11:38-44

[38]Then Jesus . . . greatly disturbed, came to the tomb [of Lazarus]. It was a cave, and a stone was lying against it. [39]Jesus said, "Take away the stone." Martha, the sister of the dead man, said to him, "Lord, already there is a stench because he has been dead four days." [40]Jesus said to her, "Did I not tell you that if you believed, you would see the glory of God?" [41]So they took away the stone. And Jesus looked upward and said, "Father, I thank you for having heard me. [42]I knew that you always hear me, but I have said this for the sake of the crowd standing here, so that they may believe that you sent me." [43]When he had said this, he cried with a loud voice, "Lazarus, come out!" [44]The dead man came out, his hands and feet bound with strips of cloth, and his face wrapped in a cloth. Jesus said to them, "Unbind him, and let him go."

1. Why do you think Jesus gives thanks to the Father before asking him to raise Lazarus? What does this imply about his confidence that the Father will answer his prayer?

   _____

   _____

   _____

   _____

   _____

2. What does Jesus' prayer say to us about the relationship we should have with our heavenly Father when we come before him with our needs?

_____

_____

_____

_____

_____

3. Jesus says, "I knew that you always hear me." Do you believe that your Father in heaven always hears your prayers? Why or why not?

_____

_____

_____

_____

_____

From the Church:

Just as Jesus prays to the Father and gives thanks before receiving his gifts, so he teaches us *filial boldness*: "Whatever you ask in prayer, believe that you receive it, and you will" (Mark 11:24). Such is the power of prayer and of faith that does not doubt: "all things are possible to him who believes" (Mark 9:23; cf. Matthew 21:22). (*Catechism,* 2610)

1. "Filial boldness" is the boldness that a child would have with his or her parent. Have you ever dared to pray with such boldness? Have you ever dared to pray for what seemed impossible? If so, what happened?

   _____

   _____

   _____

   _____

   _____

2. How can a spirit of self-sufficiency be a hindrance to prayer? What does our dependence on our Father say about our relationship with him?

   _____

   _____

   _____

   _____

   _____

3. How often do you struggle with doubts that God will give you what you need? Why is it important to trust in God when we don't see immediate answers to our prayers?

   _____

   _____

   _____

   _____

   _____

For Further Reflection and Discussion:

1. Why do you think Christians throughout the ages have accompanied their petitions with practices like fasting, going to Mass, or praying the rosary? What practices have you found helpful? How do these practices help us to unite our will to God's?

   _____

   _____

   _____

   _____

   _____

2. Do you regularly share your prayer needs with a trusted friend or family member? How may this bolster your confidence in the power of prayer? Why is it beneficial to pray together with others? (see Matthew 18:20).

   _____

   _____

   _____

   _____

   _____

3. What character traits or qualities of the heart help us to become more powerful intercessors?

   _____

   _____

   _____

   _____

4. Share a time when you personally witnessed the power of prayer. How did it affect your faith?

_____

_____

_____

_____

_____

Confidence in God's Plan for Our Lives

6

*N*one of our lives proceeds in a straight line. There are inevitably twists and turns along the way. Sometimes things don't go the way we planned, and that can leave us wondering, What is God doing in this situation? How will it all work out? However, even when we are in the midst of a situation that doesn't make sense to us, we need to have confidence that God is working in our lives and that he has a plan for us. After all, he loves us and wants to have an intimate relationship with us. His plan is always for our ultimate good: that we cooperate with him in spreading his reign on earth and that we spend eternity with him in heaven.

Susan was devastated the day her boss called her into his office and gently told her that he had to let her go. She had worked at the company for ten years and believed that she would continue to work there until she was ready to retire. For days afterward, she was numb, panicked at the thought of finding another job with equivalent pay and benefits. She also wondered why God would allow such a turn of events.

For several months, Susan spent all her time intensively looking for a new job in her field. Nothing came up, and she felt rejected and depressed. One day, while she was having lunch with a friend, she bumped into an old colleague who asked her if she would be available for consulting work. Susan jumped at the opportunity. Soon other consulting opportunities came her way. Before she knew it, Susan was working out of her home as a consultant and turning away work. Without her long commute, Susan found time and energy to pray, exercise, renew friendships, and volunteer at her parish. As she saw the quality of her life improve, Susan looked back on those long months of joblessness and realized that God's plan for her was even better than her own.

Scripture: Acts 16:11-15, 40

[11]We set sail from Troas and took a straight course to Samothrace, the following day to Neapolis, [12]and from there to Philippi, which is a leading city of the district of Macedonia and a Roman colony. We remained in this city for some days. [13]On the sabbath day we went outside the gate by the river, where we supposed there was a place of prayer; and we sat down and spoke to the women who had gathered there. [14]A certain woman named Lydia, a worshiper of God, was listening to us; she was from the city of Thyatira and a dealer in purple cloth. The Lord opened her heart to listen eagerly to what was said by Paul. [15]When she and her household were baptized, she urged us, saying, "If you have judged me to be faithful to the Lord, come and stay at my home." And she prevailed upon us. . . .

[40]After leaving the prison they went to Lydia's home; and when they had seen and encouraged the brothers and sisters there, they departed.

1. St. Paul had not been planning to visit Philippi but did so after receiving a vision of a man from Macedonia pleading with him to go there (see Acts 16:9-10). His obedience to the Holy Spirit resulted in conversion for Lydia and her household, as well as

the creation of the church at Philippi. What are some ways we can better listen to the Holy Spirit so that we are able to carry out the plans God has for us?

_____

_____

_____

_____

_____

2. A "God worshiper" was a Gentile who, although not Jewish, believed in the tenets of the Jewish faith. Lydia was at the riverbank the day St. Paul appeared because she wanted to pray with the Jewish women there. How did Lydia's initial openness to God allow him to work powerfully in her life? Share a time when you saw God's plan unfold in your own life because of your own spirit of openness.

_____

_____

_____

_____

_____

3. Purple cloth was a luxury item, so we can safely assume that Lydia was a prosperous merchant. When Lydia accepted Paul's message and was baptized, she immediately opened up her home to him. How may God be calling us to use our own possessions to serve him? How may that be part of God's plan for our lives?

_____

_____

_____

_____

_____

From the Church:

To human beings God even gives the power of freely sharing in his providence by entrusting them with the responsibility of "subduing" the earth and having dominion over it (cf. Genesis 1:26-28). God thus enables men to be intelligent and free causes in order to complete the work of creation, to perfect its harmony for their own good and that of their neighbors. Though often unconscious collaborators with God's will, they can also enter deliberately into the divine plan by their actions, their prayers, and their sufferings (cf. Colossians 1:24). They then fully be-come "God's fellow workers" and co-workers for his kingdom. (*Catechism, 307*)

1. Do you view God's plan for your life as a mission to "complete the work of creation," as defined in the *Catechism*? Why or why not?

_____

_____

_____

_____

_____

2. Can you think of a time in your life when you collaborated with God by your "actions," "prayers," or "sufferings"?

_____

_____

_____

_____

_____

3. In what ways do you see yourself as a co-worker in God's kingdom? What other ways may God be calling you to build his kingdom?

_____

_____

_____

_____

_____

For Further Reflection and Discussion:

1. Think back over the various stages of your life so far: as a child, an adolescent, a young woman, a mature woman. How did God's plan unfold in your own life in each of these times? What are you most grateful for as you look back on your life?

_____

_____

_____

_____

_____

2. Why should we be confident in God's plan for our lives, even when we don't understand it or it doesn't make sense to us? How can you continue to do the work God is calling you to do, even when you are experiencing trials or difficulties?

_____

_____

_____

_____

_____

3. Think back on a time when you might have resisted God's plan for you in order to pursue your own goals. What would you do differently? What can you do now to pursue God's goals?

_____

_____

_____

_____

_____

4. Spend some time in prayer asking God to reveal more of his plan for you. What are the desires of your heart? Are they part of God's plan for your future?

_____

_____

_____

_____

_____

Confidence in the Body of Christ

Sometimes it's easy to forget that we belong to the family of God. Through Christ's death and resurrection, we have become adopted daughters of our Father in heaven and brothers and sisters to one another. We are one body in Christ. That means we can turn to our sisters in the Lord for love and support. We need to have confidence that we can be Christ to our sisters and that they can be Christ to us.

Leslie grew up in an abusive home. As a young teenager, she began self-medicating and eventually became addicted to street drugs. The betrayal she had experienced in her family made it difficult for her to trust anyone. Whenever anyone tried to get closer to her, she backed away. Finally, after spending all her money on drugs, she lost her apartment and found herself at a shelter for the homeless. Depressed and alone, Leslie felt that God had abandoned her.

While in the shelter, Leslie met a volunteer named Sheila. Sheila seemed to enjoy chatting with Leslie and was genuinely interested in getting to know her. Leslie sometimes worried that if Sheila knew the crimes and sins she had committed, she wouldn't even talk to her. But Sheila never judged her or even asked her about those things. She was warm and joyful, especially when she talked about God. Sheila assured Leslie that God loved her and was always ready to forgive her. When Leslie was finally through drug rehab and able to find a place to live, Sheila continued to visit and encourage her. Leslie knew that God had brought Sheila into her life to show her how much he loved her.

Scripture: Acts 9:10-20

[10]Now there was a disciple in Damascus named Ananias. The Lord said to him in a vision, "Ananias." He answered, "Here I am, Lord." [11]The Lord said to him, "Get up and go to the street called Straight, and at the house of Judas look for a man of Tarsus named Saul. At this moment he is praying, [12]and he has seen in a vision a man named Ananias come in and lay his hands on him so that he might regain his sight." [13]But Ananias answered, "Lord, I have heard from many about this man, how much evil he has done to your saints in Jerusalem; [14]and here he has authority from the chief priests to bind all who invoke your name." [15]But the Lord said to him, "Go, for he is an instrument whom I have chosen to bring my name before Gentiles and kings and before the people of Israel; [16]I myself will show him how much he must suffer for the sake of my name." [17]So Ananias went and entered the house. He laid his hands on Saul and said, "Brother Saul, the Lord Jesus, who appeared to you on your way here, has sent me so that you may regain your sight and be filled with the Holy Spirit." [18]And immediately something like scales fell from his eyes, and his sight was restored. Then he got up and was baptized, [19]and after taking some food, he regained his strength.

For several days he was with the disciples in Damascus, [20]and immediately he began to proclaim Jesus in the synagogues, saying, "He is the Son of God."

1. God could have given Saul back his sight without the intervention of Ananias. Why do you think he chose Ananias to look for Saul and to pray with him?

_____

_____

_____

_____

_____

2. Ananias hesitated at first, knowing that Saul had persecuted the followers of Jesus. What enabled him to go to Saul as a brother in Christ?

_____

_____

_____

_____

_____

3. Once Saul regained his sight, he was baptized and stayed with the disciples in Damascus for several days. Why do you think it was important for Saul, soon to be called Paul, to spend time with his brothers and sisters in Christ? What do you think happened during this time?

_____

_____

_____

_____

_____

From the Church:

Now the Father's will is "to raise up men to share in his own divine life." He does this by gathering men around his Son Jesus Christ. This gathering is the Church. . . . Christ stands at the heart of this gathering of men into the "family of God" . . . Jesus calls all people to come together around him. . . . Into this union with Christ all men are called. (*Catechism*, 541, 542)

1. Have you ever viewed the body of Christ, the church, as a "gathering" around Jesus? How does this image help you to see the body of Christ in a new or different way?

_____

_____

_____

_____

_____

2. How often do you think of other Christians as your brothers and sisters in Christ? What difference would it make in your life to consider other believers as members of your family?

_____

_____

_____

_____

_____

3. When we are in union with Christ, we share one divine life with our brothers and sisters. What are some tangible, practical, everyday ways that we can share our lives with those in the body? What may be holding us back from doing so?

_____

_____

_____

_____

_____

For Further Reflection and Discussion:

1. How can our culture's values of individualism and independence at times prevent us from fully living as one body, united in Christ?

_____

_____

_____

_____

_____

2. How does sharing our lives in Christ enrich our relationships? How does being Christian enrich our relationships with those who are not believers?

_____

_____

_____

_____

_____

3. What obstacles have at times prevented you from seeing other Christians as your brothers and sisters? What can you do to overcome such obstacles?

_____

_____

_____

_____

_____

4. In what ways have you felt supported in your Christian life by other Christians? How can you be a better support to the Christians you encounter each day, especially those who are needy?

_____

_____

_____

_____

_____

Confidence in Eternal Life

God's promise of eternal life! We all want to hold on to that promise, especially when we lose a loved one or face the prospect of our own death. While there is no sure way of knowing what life after death will be like, the deeper our experience of the reality of God is in this life, the stronger our confidence will be in the reality of the next life. After all, life with God is what we are created for, both now on earth and forever in heaven.

The decision to hold on to God's promise is especially important when we are faced with an unexpected loss. The decision to trust in God's promise of eternal life kept Carol going when she lost her seven-year-old daughter, Katie, literally overnight. Katie went to bed with a cold, and she died during the night of an acute viral infection that closed off her air passages. Carol was in such a state of shock and grief that she didn't know if she could live through the tragedy. Each day, when she woke up and realized that her precious daughter was gone, she wanted to turn over and go back to sleep, hoping that it was all a bad dream or that she would die, too, ending her misery.

In her agony, Carol cried out to the Lord, and he gave her a special gift. One night, about a month after Katie had died, Carol had a dream about her daughter. Katie was holding someone's hand, and she said to Carol, "Mommy, I'm with God." The dream helped Carol to believe that when Katie died that night, never to wake up again in her own bed, she awoke in the arms of God. The experience filled her with the hope she needed to survive. She could go on with her life, as she looked forward to the time one day when she would be reunited once again with her daughter.

Scripture: 2 Maccabees 7:1-2, 20-23

[1]It happened also that seven brothers and their mother were arrested and were being compelled by the king, under torture with whips and thongs, to partake of unlawful swine's flesh. [2]One of them, acting as their spokesman, said, "What do you intend to ask and learn from us? For we are ready to die rather than transgress the laws of our ancestors." . . .

[20]The mother was especially admirable and worthy of honorable memory. Although she saw her seven sons perish within a single day, she bore it with good courage because of her hope in the Lord. [21]She encouraged each of them in the language of their ancestors. Filled with a noble spirit, she reinforced her woman's reasoning with a man's courage, and said to them, [22]"I do not know how you came into being in my womb. It was not I who gave you life and breath, nor I who set in order the elements within each of you. [23]Therefore the Creator of the world, who shaped the beginning of humankind and devised the origin of all things, will in his mercy give life and breath back to you again, since you now forget yourselves for the sake of his laws."

1. Why do you think the mother in Maccabees was so confident that her sons would be raised up to life again? What was her reasoning?

_____

_____

_____

_____

_____

2. How did the mother view life? Why did she place her hope in God?

_____

_____

_____

_____

_____

3. Why are martyrs such a positive witness of everlasting life? How can our own faith in eternal life be a witness to others who struggle with doubts about life after death?

_____

_____

_____

_____

_____

From the Church:

United with Christ by Baptism, believers already truly participate in the heavenly life of the risen Christ, but this life remains "hidden with Christ in God" (Colossians 3:3; cf. Philippians 4:23). . . . When we rise on the last day we "also will appear with him in glory" (Colossians 3:4). (*Catechism,* 1003)

This perfect life with the Most Holy Trinity—this communion of life and love with the Trinity, with the Virgin Mary, the angels and all the blessed—is called "heaven." Heaven is the ultimate end and fulfillment of the deepest human longings, the state of supreme, definitive happiness. (*Catechism,* 1024)

1. What are your images of heaven? How are they similar to or different from the description of heaven given in the *Catechism?*

_____

_____

_____

_____

_____

2. What is your "deepest human longing"? How do you think it will be fulfilled in heaven?

_____

_____

_____

_____

_____

3. Think about the resurrection appearances of Jesus to Mary Magdalene (John 20:11-18), to the apostle Thomas (John 20:26-29), on the road to Emmaus (Luke 24:13-35), and by the sea, eating breakfast with Peter and the apostles (John 21:1-14). Based on these passages, what do you think it will be like to have a resurrected body? Imagine what it will be like to live in a world that is a new creation, where Christ appears in his glory.

_____

_____

_____

_____

_____

For Further Reflection and Discussion:

1. What are some concrete ways that you experience "heaven on earth"? What is it about these experiences that makes them a foretaste of heaven?

_____

_____

_____

_____

_____

2. If you knew that you had only a few weeks to live, what would you do to prepare for your death? What can you do now that will help you be ready for that day?

_____

_____

_____

_____

_____

3. Do you believe that the saints and your deceased loved ones in heaven can intercede for you? Do you pray to them? How would a greater understanding of the Catholic teaching of the communion of saints help you to place your hope in their prayers for you? (see *Catechism*, 946–48).

_____

_____

_____

_____

_____

4. Spend some time in prayer, meditating on the experience of entering heaven. Imagine being joyfully greeted by the Lord and being reunited with your loved ones. How might such a prayer combat any fears or anxiety you may have about death?

_____

_____

_____

_____

_____

Part Two

Confidence in God's Call in Our Lives

Confidence in Our Humanity

Have you ever thought of yourself as a "new creation"? When Christ died for us, our old selves died with him. Through his death and resurrection, we have been reborn. We now have something new in us—God's life! Of course, we know that we aren't perfect; daily we still struggle with faults and imperfections. But God loved us even before we became a new creation—so much so that he sent his only Son to bring us his life. If he has accepted our own frail humanity, so should we! He loves us with all our weaknesses and human frailties, and we can abide with him without fear that we aren't perfect yet. Each day he calls us to himself to receive more of his life—that life that has the power to change us to become more like him.

Mary had always had a poor opinion of herself. Deep down, she believed that she was fundamentally flawed. Whenever she got angry at her husband or children or fearful or anxious about their finances, she beat herself up. She believed that she should always be patient, courageous, and calm. And she often worried about what other people thought of her. Everyone else she knew seemed to have a better handle on their emotions and their lives.

After years of struggling with these negative feelings about herself, Mary found herself in a full-fledged depression. Barely able to get out of bed each morning, she sought counseling and medication. When a friend invited her to a healing Mass, she hesitated but then decided to go. To her surprise, the priest's homily seemed to be meant just for her. The truth, he said, is that none of us measures up. We all fall short of the glory of God. But in Christ, we are a new creation. He can renew our humanity and make us into his own image. As Mary listened, she felt a glimmer of hope. She realized that her negative thinking was leaving Christ out of the equation. What he had done through his cross and resurrection had meaning for her life, here and now. As she drew close to him and clung to him, Christ could replace her negative ways of thinking of herself with the truth. Her dignity and value flowed from God. She was his beloved daughter.

When a member of the healing prayer team prayed over her, she felt God's love wash over her. That evening was a turning point in her life. She knew, at the core of her being, that God loved her just as she was, with all her weaknesses. It was useless to measure herself against some false standard of perfection. Her Father wanted her to spend time with him each day, and the more time she spent with him, the more she would take on his loving, merciful nature.

Scripture: 2 Corinthians 5:14-17

[14]For the love of Christ urges us on, because we are convinced that one has died for all; therefore all have died. [15]And he died for all, so that those who live might live no longer for themselves, but for him who died and was raised for them.

[16]From now on, therefore, we regard no one from a human point of view; even though we once knew Christ from a human point of view, we know him no longer in that way. [17]So if anyone is in Christ, there is a new creation: everything old has passed away; see, everything has become new!

1. Why does St. Paul say that in Christ, "everything old has passed away" (verse 17)? How does knowing and experiencing God's love help us to put to death our "old selves" and put on the "new"? (see Ephesians 4:22-24).

_____

_____

_____

_____

_____

2. How often do you regard things from a "human point of view" (verse 16), rather than from God's viewpoint? What difference would it make if you viewed yourself with God's eyes, rather than with your own?

_____

_____

_____

_____

_____

3. How do you live "in Christ" (verse 17)? What does living in Christ require of you?

_____

_____

_____

_____

_____

From the Church:

Man cannot live without love. He remains a being that is incomprehensible for himself, his life is senseless, if love is not revealed to him, if he does not encounter love, if he does not experience it and make it his own, if he does not participate intimately in it. This . . . is why Christ the Redeemer "fully reveals man to himself." If we may use the expression, this is the human dimension of the mystery of the Redemption. In this dimension man finds again the greatness, dignity and value that belong to his humanity. In the mystery of the Redemption man becomes newly "expressed" and, in a way, is newly created. He is newly created!
. . . The man who wishes to understand himself thoroughly—and not just in accordance with immediate, partial, often superficial, and even illusory standards and measures of his being—he must with his unrest, uncertainty and even his weakness and sinfulness, with his life and death, draw near to Christ. He must, so to speak, enter into him with all his own self, he must "appropriate" and assimilate the whole of the reality of the Incarnation and Redemption in order to find himself. If this profound process takes place within him, he then bears fruit not only of adoration of God but also of deep wonder at himself. (Pope John Paul II, *Redemptor hominis*, 10)

1. Christ the Redeemer "fully reveals man to himself." In what ways does Jesus help you discover more about yourself?

_____

_____

_____

_____

_____

2. How often are you tempted to take a dim view of humanity? Why do we need Christ's redemption to discover the greatness, dignity, and value that belong to us?

_____

_____

_____

_____

3. What meaning does the incarnation have in your life? How might the fact that God became incarnate in Jesus lead you to arrive at a place of "deep wonder" of yourself?

_____

_____

_____

_____

_____

For Further Reflection and Discussion:

1. Our feelings about ourselves are often a reflection of how we were raised. How can a deeper understanding of ourselves as new creations in Christ help us overcome the negative messages we might have received about ourselves while we were growing up?

_____

_____

_____

_____

_____

2. St. Paul tells us to "be renewed in the spirit of [our] minds" by putting off our old selves and putting on our new selves (Ephesians 4:22-24). What do you think it means to renew our minds? What are some practical ways to do so?

_____

_____

_____

_____

_____

3. Why is it important to accept all dimensions of our humanity, even those that we struggle with? Why is it important to make a distinction between accepting our weaknesses and excusing them? How do you think Jesus wants us to deal with our human weaknesses?

_____

_____

_____

_____

_____

4. How can loving ourselves in Christ be an act of gratitude and a sign of reverence and awe, rather than a sin of pride?

_____

_____

_____

_____

Confidence in Our Femininity

What does it mean to be a woman today? How are we to express our femininity in our relationships, in our families, and in the world? Controversy and new thinking about gender have led to much confusion. For example, are "traditional" feminine characteristics due to our upbringing, or do they go deeper to how God created us? How are we to be confident of our femininity without appearing weak or inferior?

To discover what it means to be feminine requires that we go back to the beginning—to Genesis. In those passages, we learn that God created humans "in his image, . . . male and female he created them" (1:27). We were created by God as women, equal to but different from men. As women, we reflect the image of God to the same degree as men. Original sin tainted the relationship between men and women. But domination of men over women is not what God intended. The Lord wants men and women to live as equals and in the special communion of marriage as "one flesh." Whether or not we are currently married, our dignity derives from the fact that we were created to love and to make a sincere gift of ourselves in love to our families and to whomever we encounter each day.

For years, Jennifer had worked for a local retailer, many of whose employees were women. After many promotions, she found herself working with other executives, all of whom were men. In this atmosphere, Jennifer feared that her male colleagues would not take her seriously unless she adopted a more aggressive style. However, her often abrupt and harsh mannerisms damaged many of her working relationships. She found herself increasingly isolated at work and unhappy.

One day while she was attending a retreat for women, Jennifer met another woman named Donna who also worked in a high-level position, mostly with men. Donna seemed relaxed and approachable. As they spent time over lunch, Jennifer felt safe expressing some of her frustrations about her work environment. Donna sympathized but urged Jennifer to be confident that God would give her all the skills and wisdom she would need to do her job. She did not have to sacrifice her God-given feminine qualities in order to do her job well. In fact, Donna said, the more she was truly herself, the more effective she would be in her job.

Scripture: Proverbs 31:10-31

[10]A capable wife who can find?
  She is far more precious than jewels.
[11]The heart of her husband trusts in her,
  and he will have no lack of gain.
[12]She does him good, and not harm,
  all the days of her life.
[13]She seeks wool and flax,
  and works with willing hands.
[14]She is like the ships of the merchant,
  she brings her food from far away.
[15]She rises while it is still night

and provides food for her household
and tasks for her servant-girls.
¹⁶She considers a field and buys it;
with the fruit of her hands she plants a vineyard.
¹⁷She girds herself with strength,
and makes her arms strong.
¹⁸She perceives that her merchandise is profitable.
Her lamp does not go out at night.
¹⁹She puts her hands to the distaff,
and her hands hold the spindle.
²⁰She opens her hand to the poor,
and reaches out her hands to the needy.
²¹She is not afraid for her household when it snows,
for all her household are clothed in crimson.
²²She makes herself coverings;
her clothing is fine linen and purple.
²³Her husband is known in the city gates,
taking his seat among the elders of the land.
²⁴She makes linen garments and sells them;
she supplies the merchant with sashes.
²⁵Strength and dignity are her clothing,
and she laughs at the time to come.
²⁶She opens her mouth with wisdom,
and the teaching of kindness is on her tongue.
²⁷She looks well to the ways of her household,
and does not eat the bread of idleness.
²⁸Her children rise up and call her happy;
her husband too, and he praises her:
²⁹"Many women have done excellently,
but you surpass them all."
³⁰Charm is deceitful, and beauty is vain,
but a woman who fears the LORD is to be praised.
³¹Give her a share in the fruit of her hands,
and let her works praise her in the city gates.

1. What qualities do you most admire in the woman described in these verses? In what specific ways does she show love for her family and for others? In what ways does she exhibit strength?

_____

_____

_____

_____

_____

2. Do you think this woman considers herself an equal of her husband? Why or why not?

_____

_____

_____

_____

3. How does the woman of Proverbs 31 show confidence in her femininity? In her role as wife, mother, and breadwinner?

_____

_____

_____

_____

From the Church:

Man and woman have been *created*, which is to say, *willed* by God: on the one hand, in perfect equality as human persons; on the other, in their respective beings as man and woman. . . . Man and woman are both with one and the same dignity "in the image of God." In their "being-man" and "being-woman," they reflect the Creator's wisdom and goodness. (*Catechism*, 369)
Man and woman were made "for each other" . . . in which each can be "helpmate" to the other, for they are equal as persons . . . and complementary as masculine and feminine. (*Catechism*, 372)

1. What kind of messages do women sometimes receive in their families or in society that may lead them to believe that they are inferior to men? How does the creation story repudiate such thinking?

   _____

   _____

   _____

   _____

   _____

2. How do human beings, created as man and woman, reflect God's wisdom and goodness? How do men and women complement one another?

   _____

   _____

   _____

   _____

   _____

3. Why do you think society often portrays men and women as working against each other? How can men and women better complement one another, rather than acting as adversaries?

_____

_____

_____

_____

_____

For Further Reflection and Discussion:

1. What kinds of messages were communicated to you about the dignity of women as you were growing up? What impact did they have on you later, as an adult?

_____

_____

_____

_____

_____

2. How is femininity portrayed in the media? How can a false notion of femininity lead women to place too much value on how they look?

_____

_____

_____

_____

_____

3. What are some characteristics of women that seem to be unique to their feminine nature? What do these characteristics contribute to the family? To the workplace? To the world?

_____

_____

_____

_____

_____

4. What can you do to help teens and young women have a sense of their worth and dignity? What can you do or say that would encourage them to have confidence in their femininity?

_____

_____

_____

_____

_____

Confidence in Our Vocation

*A*s daughters of our heavenly Father who are baptized into Christ, we all have the same vocation: to love God and to reflect his love to the world. We are called to live out this fundamental vocation in a specific state in life, whether that be as married, single, consecrated, or religious. Whatever our vocation, God gives us the grace to live it out.

When Marilyn married her high school sweetheart, Steve, at the age of twenty, she thought they would live together "happily ever after." Looking back, Marilyn realized that she was naïve and a bit starry-eyed. The usual struggles of married life were soon upon them. Tension over money, kids, and basic differences in how they approached life came to a head five years later, and Steve moved out of the house for a few weeks. However, neither Marilyn nor Steve wanted to give up on their marriage. With the help of counseling and prayer, they were gradually able to rebuild their life together.

As Marilyn learned more about her faith, she realized that marriage was the vocation God had given to her to live out her baptismal vows. It was the means for both Steve and her to grow in holiness. Because her marriage was a sacrament and God's gift to Steve and her, she knew that the Lord would not let them down. As they stayed close to him, he brought joy into their marriage, even as he helped them through the rough spots.

Scripture: Luke 2:22-24, 36-39

²²When the time came for their purification according to the law of Moses, they [Mary and Joseph] brought him [Jesus] up to Jerusalem to present him to the Lord ²³(as it is written in the law of the Lord, "Every firstborn male shall be designated as holy to the Lord"), ²⁴and they offered a sacrifice according to what is stated in the law of the Lord, "a pair of turtledoves or two young pigeons." . . .

³⁶There was also a prophet, Anna the daughter of Phanuel, of the tribe of Asher. She was of a great age, having lived with her husband seven years after her marriage, ³⁷then as a widow to the age of eighty-four. She never left the temple but worshiped there with fasting and prayer night and day. ³⁸At that moment she came, and began to praise God and to speak about the child to all who were looking for the redemption of Jerusalem.

³⁹When they had finished everything required by the law of the Lord, they returned to Galilee, to their own town of Nazareth.

1. How confident do you think Mary and Joseph felt about their vocation? What previous experiences might have helped them to place their trust in God for help in living out his unique call to them?

_____

_____

_____

_____

_____

2. What actions did Mary and Joseph take in this Scripture passage that flowed out of their vocations? How can our God-given vocations give our lives direction and meaning?

_____

_____

_____

_____

_____

3. How did Anna take advantage of her state of widowhood to serve God? Why do you think she was able to recognize Jesus as the Messiah?

_____

_____

_____

_____

_____

From the Church:

God who created man out of love also calls him to love—the fundamental and innate vocation of every human being. For man is created in the image and likeness of God who is himself love. Since God created him man and woman, their mutual love becomes an image of the absolute and unfailing love with which God loves man. (*Catechism*, 1604)

Both the sacrament of Matrimony and virginity for the Kingdom of God come from the Lord himself. It is he who gives them meaning and grants them the grace which is indispensable for living them out in conformity with his will. (*Catechism,* 1620)

1. What is the main purpose of your life? How does the call to love contrast with the world's assumptions—and even our own— about what our purpose in life should be?

_____

_____

_____

_____

_____

2. Why is it important to understand that God gives meaning to both marriage and the single life? How does a deeper understanding of the meaning of our vocations help us to live them out in a way that is pleasing to God?

_____

_____

_____

_____

_____

3. How often have you viewed your vocation as a gift? How can looking at your state in life as a gift from God help you in living out his call to you?

_____

_____

_____

_____

For Further Reflection and Discussion:

1. Some women desire marriage but never meet the right person. Other women are divorced or widowed. How can women embrace a vocation as a single person, even if that is not what they had desired for their lives?

_____

_____

_____

_____

_____

2. Why do you think the church talks about vocations? Why is it important to teach our children and the other young people in our lives that God may have a specific "assignment" to give them?

_____

_____

_____

_____

3. Share a time when God gave you wisdom or strength to fulfill your vocation. When did you recognize God's intervention? How did this build your confidence in him and in the vocation he has given you?

_____

_____

_____

_____

4. What has been the greatest blessing of living out your vocation? What joys have come specifically from God's call to you?

_____

_____

_____

_____

_____

Confidence in Our Call to Holiness

12

When we try to think of ourselves as holy, often our first reaction is to exclaim, "Not me!" That may be because we tend to think of holiness as something reserved for great saints and heroes, and we know we aren't in *that* category! However, the truth is that by the fact of our baptism we are *all* called to holiness. So, what does holiness look like? It's often helpful to think about holy people who are living very ordinary lives. When we do, we realize that it's not the greatness of what we do that matters but the love with which we do it.

When Jane and her husband, Tom, moved into a new apartment building, they met their elderly next-door neighbor Rose, who welcomed them to the building and invited them over for a glass of wine. As they sat and talked, she told them about her life. She was a widow who was struggling with some health issues, but she was still involved in her parish and went to daily Mass. Her ministry was to reach out to shut-ins in the parish by sending them cards and notes and by calling them on the phone. She seemed genuinely interested in Jane and Tom, and they both felt relaxed and comfortable with her. They soon became good friends. Jane and Tom viewed Rose as a quiet but strong support in their lives. She always inquired how they were and what needs they had that she could pray for. She spoke about God as if he were her closest friend. It was clear that throughout her life she had always leaned on the Lord and enjoyed a rich and rewarding relationship with him.

When Rose died suddenly two years later, Jane and Tom knew they had lost a dear and special friend. Rose had truly inspired them to draw closer to the Lord themselves. At her funeral, they were surprised to hear from many people whose lives Rose had also touched in her quiet but powerful way. When the parish priest described Rose as a holy person who now was seeing God face to face, Jane and Tom knew they had an advocate in heaven who would continue to intercede for their needs.

Scripture: Matthew 5:14-16, 1 Thessalonians 3:12-13

5:14[Jesus said,] "You are the light of the world. A city built on a hill cannot be hid. 15No one after lighting a lamp puts it under the bushel basket, but on the lampstand, and it gives light to all in the house. 16In the same way, let your light shine before others, so that they may see your good works and give glory to your Father in heaven."

3:12May the Lord make you increase and abound in love for one another and for all, just as we abound in love for you. 13And may he so strengthen your hearts in holiness that you may be blameless before our God and Father at the coming of our Lord Jesus with all his saints.

1. Based on Jesus' words, what is the reason God calls us to be holy? How do our holiness and our love for God affect others?

_____

_____

_____

_____

_____

2. Why does Jesus tell his followers that they are the light of the world? When have you been a "light" in your home, your workplace, or your parish? In what specific ways can you bring more of Christ's light into the world?

_____

_____

_____

_____

_____

3. According to St. Paul, who makes us holy? Why do you think it's important to ask God for the strength and grace to become holy and blameless before God?

_____

_____

_____

_____

_____

From the Church:

Fortified by so many and such powerful means of salvation, all the faithful, whatever their condition or state, are called by the Lord, each in his own way, to that perfect holiness whereby the Father Himself is perfect. (Vatican II, _Lumen gentium_, 11)

Healing the wounds of sin, the Holy Spirit renews us interiorly through a spiritual transformation. He enlightens and strengthens us to live as "children of light" through "all that is good and right and true." (*Catechism*, 1695)

1. The Second Vatican Council's document *Lumen gentium* (which means "Light to the Nations") said that all Christians, whether religious or lay, are called to holiness. This means that whatever our state of life, we can find opportunities to become holy. What opportunities can you find in your daily life to grow in holiness?

_____

_____

_____

_____

2. How does the Holy Spirit empower us to live a holy life? What does his presence within us do for us?

_____

_____

_____

_____

3. Think of a moment or an incident in which you were aware of the Holy Spirit's working within you to bring you closer to your heavenly Father or to conquer a temptation. What happened?

_____

_____

_____

_____

_____

For Further Reflection and Discussion:

1. Think of one or two people you know whom you consider holy. What qualities do they possess? Based on their example, how would you define "holiness"?

_____

_____

_____

_____

_____

2. Why does holiness consist of more than avoidance of sin? How may the Lord be calling you to holiness through prayer or service?

_____

_____

_____

_____

_____

3. Why is it important for us to be forgiving of ourselves when we miss opportunities to be holy? What's the best way to move forward when we have failed?

_____

_____

_____

_____

_____

4. Think of several Scripture verses that might help you remember God's call to holiness. Share them with your group and explain why you chose them. Then write them on sticky notes or index cards, and place them around your home where you will see them each day.

_____

_____

_____

_____

Confidence in Our Talents

Why do we need to have confidence in our talents? Without the recognition of our gifts and the desire to develop them, God can't use us for his purposes. We all have a unique and specific role to play in God's kingdom. When we fail to develop or exercise our gifts—for whatever reason—then the work God has for us may never be accomplished! The more we step out in faith in developing and exercising our gifts, the more God will use us to build his kingdom.

Sheila grew up in a single-parent, low-income home. In high school, the many hours she had to work at various part-time jobs left her little time to focus on her studies, and consequently she didn't earn high grades. After graduation, she got a full-time job serving tables at a local restaurant.

One day the owner of the restaurant approached Sheila and asked her if she was interested in becoming a manager. Sheila hesitated. She didn't think she was capable of taking on such responsibility. What if she took the position and then discovered that she couldn't do it? She thanked him for the offer but said that she didn't think the job was for her.

Several months later, the owner approached her again with the same offer. He told her that he was impressed with the way she interacted with the customers and with the other staff. He believed she could do the job and do it well. This time Sheila decided to give it a try. After a few weeks of training, she plunged in. There were definitely moments when she felt panicked and wondered how to handle a new or difficult situation. Each time, she sent up a quick prayer to God for wisdom, and each time he helped her through.

As Sheila's confidence increased, so did her management skills. She realized that God had given her gifts in this area and that she should develop them for his glory. With the encouragement of the owner, she decided to take classes at the local community college. Sheila eventually earned a college degree. Then she took a position managing volunteers and fundraising at a local nonprofit agency that helped single mothers with job training and employment.

Scripture: Acts 18:1-4, 18-19, 24-28

[1]After this Paul left Athens and went to Corinth. [2]There he found a Jew named Aquila, a native of Pontus, who had recently come from Italy with his wife Priscilla, because Claudius had ordered all Jews to leave Rome. Paul went to see them, [3]and, because he was of the same trade, he stayed with them, and they worked together—by trade they were tentmakers. [4]Every sabbath he would argue in the synagogue and would try to convince Jews and Greeks. . . .

[18]After staying there for a considerable time, Paul said farewell to the believers and sailed for Syria, accompanied by Priscilla and Aquila. At Cenchreae he had his hair cut, for he was under a vow. [19]When they reached Ephesus, he left them there. . . .

[24]Now there came to Ephesus a Jew named Apollos, a native of Alexandria. He was an eloquent man, well-versed in the scrip-

tures. [25]He had been instructed in the Way of the Lord; and he spoke with burning enthusiasm and taught accurately the things concerning Jesus, though he knew only the baptism of John. [26]He began to speak boldly in the synagogue; but when Priscilla and Aquila heard him, they took him aside and explained the Way of God to him more accurately. [27]And when he wished to cross over to Achaia, the believers encouraged him and wrote to the disciples to welcome him. On his arrival he greatly helped those who through grace had become believers, [28]for he powerfully refuted the Jews in public, showing by the scriptures that the Messiah is Jesus.

1. Why do you think Aquila and Priscilla set sail with Paul in order to accompany him on his missionary journey? Do you think they might have doubted that they had the gifts and talents to become missionaries? If so, what might have convinced them to go?

_____

_____

_____

_____

_____

2. What effect did Aquila and Priscilla have on Apollos? How did their actions demonstrate that they had confidence in God's gifts to them?

_____

_____

_____

_____

_____

3. What talent of Apollos did God use to spread the faith? How was that talent nurtured and developed?

_____

_____

_____

_____

_____

From the Church:

The "talents" are not distributed equally. . . . These differences belong to God's plan, who wills that each receive what he needs from others, and that those endowed with particular "talents" share the benefits with those who need them. These differences encourage and often oblige persons to practice generosity, kindness, and sharing of goods. (*Catechism,* 1936, 1937)

1. Why is it important to use the talents God gives us? What happens when we fail to use our talents?

_____

_____

_____

_____

2. Why does God give different talents to different people? Why is it important to keep this truth in mind when considering what our own talents may be?

_____

_____

_____

_____

_____

3. How often do you think of your talents in relation to yourself rather than to others? How can a focus on others in assessing your talents give you more confidence in yourself and your gifts?

_____

_____

_____

_____

For Further Reflection and Discussion:

1. Do you have trouble identifying your gifts? Why or why not? Looking over your life, how have you been able to develop your natural gifts?

_____

_____

_____

_____

2. Are there gifts you have developed that don't come naturally to you? If so, how were you able to develop these gifts? In what ways can you rely more on the Lord for the gifts you still think you need?

_____

_____

_____

_____

_____

3. Have you ever asked the Lord how he wants you to use your gifts in service to the body of Christ? If you asked him that question, what might he say to you?

_____

_____

_____

_____

_____

4. How can you encourage the young people in your life to see their talents and potential careers as gifts from God to build his kingdom? How does such a view differ from how the secular world views career choices and development?

_____

_____

_____

_____

_____

Confidence in Our Call to Love One Another

14

"Love one another as I have loved you" (John 15:12). Our love for others is a response to the love that God has for us. We are called to love others with the heart of God, with his mercy, compassion, and care. It's not always easy to love other people—especially those we live with day in and day out. But when we willingly lay down our lives for others, when we easily forgive and refuse to harbor resentments, and when we avoid the temptation to control or manipulate, then our love becomes a powerful blessing and a reflection of the love of God. Each day we must place our confidence in Jesus' call to love one another as he loves us, and with his grace, to love others as Jesus loves them.

Janice had always had a tense relationship with her mother, Mary, but over the years she learned to ignore or brush aside Mary's critical comments about her husband, her children, and her home. However, Janice also purposefully limited the time she spent with her mother so that she wouldn't have to hear the criticism.

Then Mary broke her hip and could no longer live by herself. Janice's husband suggested that Mary move in with them. Janice's initial reaction was an emphatic no. How could she find the time to care for her mother? And how would she react to her mother's criticisms? But when Janice prayed about the issue, she heard the Lord gently asking her to be open to the idea.

The first few weeks after Mary moved in were difficult for everyone in the family. Janice knew right away that she would have to be honest with her mother and let her know how much her negative comments hurt. When they sat down one afternoon and Janice told her how she felt, Mary's reaction surprised her. Instead of being defensive, she broke down and cried. Through her tears, Mary asked for forgiveness and said that she hadn't been aware of the effects of her words. She asked Janice to help her by telling her when she was being critical or unkind.

The next two years were both a challenge and blessing. As she cared for her mother, Janice found her patience tried many times. But she and Mary also grew closer as they learned to be forgiving with each other, to let go of past hurts, and to be honest with their feelings. When her mother passed away, Janice was grateful for the time and grace they had been given to repair their relationship and truly learn to love one another.

Scripture: Luke 10:25-37

²⁵Just then a lawyer stood up to test Jesus. "Teacher," he said, "what must I do to inherit eternal life?" ²⁶He said to him, "What is written in the law? What do you read there?" ²⁷He answered, "You shall love the Lord your God with all your heart, and with all your soul, and with all your strength, and with all your mind; and your neighbor as yourself." ²⁸And he said to him, "You have given the right answer; do this, and you will live."

²⁹But wanting to justify himself, he asked Jesus, "And who is my neighbor?" ³⁰Jesus replied, "A man was going down from Jerusalem to Jericho, and fell into the hands of robbers, who stripped him, beat him, and went away, leaving him half dead. ³¹Now by chance a priest was going down that road; and when he saw him, he passed by on the other side. ³²So likewise a Lev-

ite, when he came to the place and saw him, passed by on the other side. [33]But a Samaritan while traveling came near him; and when he saw him, he was moved with pity. [34]He went to him and bandaged his wounds, having poured oil and wine on them. Then he put him on his own animal, brought him to an inn, and took care of him. [35]The next day he took out two denarii, gave them to the innkeeper, and said, 'Take care of him; and when I come back, I will repay you whatever more you spend.' [36]Which of these three, do you think, was a neighbor to the man who fell into the hands of the robbers?" [37]He said, "The one who showed him mercy." Jesus said to him, "Go and do likewise."

1. Samaritans were viewed as enemies of the Jews. Why is it significant that the Samaritan—rather than the priest or the Levite—is the hero in this parable? What does this tell us about reaching out to others in love?

_____

_____

_____

_____

_____

2. How did the Samaritan show his commitment to the victim in the story? Why is commitment the basis for our caring for one another?

_____

_____

_____

_____

_____

3. In this story, love is an action, not an emotion. Why is it important as Christians to think of love first as an action?

_____

_____

_____

_____

_____

From the Church:

Christ died out of love for us, while we were still "enemies" (Romans 5:10). The Lord asks us to love as he does, even our *enemies*, to make ourselves the neighbor of those farthest away, and to love children and the poor as Christ himself. (*Catechism*, 1825)

1. Why does loving others often require us to "die to self"? What are some ways you have been called to die to your own desires to better serve and love someone close to you?

_____

_____

_____

_____

_____

2. Think of someone in your everyday life who irritates you in some way. How can you change the way you think about that person in order to love him or her as Christ does?

_____

_____

_____

_____

_____

3. Some attitudes we harbor may prevent us from carrying out Jesus' commandment to "love one another as I have loved you" (John 15:12). These could be self-centeredness, a lack of compassion for the needs around us, a critical or judgmental spirit, fear of rejection, or fear of the cost involved in time and effort. What attitudes may be hindering you from loving others as God desires?

_____

_____

_____

_____

For Further Reflection and Discussion:

1. In what ways do you express your love to others? For example, do you show physical affection or affirm people verbally? Do you give gifts or perform little acts of service? What other ways could you express your love that don't necessarily come naturally to you?

_____

_____

_____

_____

2. Who are the people in your life that you find most difficult to love? What prayer can you offer up to Jesus to give you a heart of love for these individuals? How can Confession help?

_____

_____

_____

_____

_____

3. Jesus often showed his love and concern for others by speaking a difficult word of correction. Do you sometimes find it difficult to correct someone or be honest with your feelings, even if you know it would be the most loving thing to do? How can you speak the truth in love?

_____

_____

_____

_____

_____

4. When we love someone, we can be tempted to become controlling because we want the best for him or her. Why is true love not controlling? How can we love others while at the same time respecting their freedom?

_____

_____

_____

_____

_____

Confidence in Our Call to Work for Justice

$\mathcal{I}$n a world filled with injustices, Christians are called to be a light in the darkness and a force for change. Yet what a challenge! Social problems and issues are so numerous that we often feel overwhelmed and don't know where to start. And we can be so wrapped up in our own affairs that we don't even notice or care about the injustices happening right in our backyards. In the end, we need to rely on the Holy Spirit to open our eyes and direct our actions. As we pray and stay close to God, he will show us what we can do, one step at a time, to make a difference.

When Georgia's neighbor asked her to help out at the local homeless shelter, she was happy to do so. She had always wanted to help people who were less fortunate than she was, and this seemed to be the perfect opportunity. But during her first visit, she was shocked to encounter not only homeless men and women, but also entire families with young children. When Georgia asked why so many families were at the shelter, she discovered that there was simply not enough subsidized or low-cost housing in her area for even the working poor to afford.

Georgia kept returning to the shelter to help, and each time she felt more passionate about the housing problem. As she prayed about it, she thought God might be calling her to become involved. She contacted her local government to find out what could be done to help these families. They referred her to a local activist group that worked to raise awareness about the lack of housing for low-income families and to urge government officials and local developers to do something about it. Soon Georgia was spending much of her spare time at the office of the community group. With the aid of her pastor, she also formed a parish committee to help a needy family find suitable housing.

Sometimes Georgia felt discouraged, since it was difficult to see whether or not her work was bearing fruit. But when she talked to her pastor, he reassured her that this was the work that God wanted her to do to build his kingdom on earth.

Scripture: Luke 16:19-31

[19]"There was a rich man who was dressed in purple and fine linen and who feasted sumptuously every day. [20]And at his gate lay a poor man named Lazarus, covered with sores, [21]who longed to satisfy his hunger with what fell from the rich man's table; even the dogs would come and lick his sores. [22]The poor man died and was carried away by the angels to be with Abraham. The rich man also died and was buried. [23]In Hades, where he was being tormented, he looked up and saw Abraham far away with Lazarus by his side. [24]He called out, 'Father Abraham, have mercy on me, and send Lazarus to dip the tip of his finger in water and cool my tongue; for I am in agony in these flames.' [25]But Abraham said, 'Child, remember that during your lifetime you received your good things, and Lazarus in like manner evil things; but now he is comforted here, and you are in agony. [26]Besides all this, between you and us a great chasm has been fixed, so that those who might want to pass from here to you cannot do so, and no one can cross from there to us.' [27]He said,

'Then, father, I beg you to send him to my father's house—²⁸for I have five brothers—that he may warn them, so that they will not also come into this place of torment.' ²⁹Abraham replied, 'They have Moses and the prophets; they should listen to them.' ³⁰He said, 'No, father Abraham; but if someone goes to them from the dead, they will repent.' ³¹He said to him, 'If they do not listen to Moses and the prophets, neither will they be convinced even if someone rises from the dead.'"

1. Why do you think Jesus told this parable to his listeners? How might this story have imparted a sense of urgency? What might have been the crowd's reaction?

_____

_____

_____

_____

_____

2. In this parable, do you think the rich man made a conscious decision to ignore Lazarus and his needs? What does this parable say about our duty to be aware of the needs of others?

_____

_____

_____

_____

_____

3. How can we become more sensitized to the suffering and needs of other people? What needs may currently exist in our own families that we are not addressing?

_____

_____

_____

_____

From the Church:

Christian revelation . . . leads us to a deeper understanding of the laws of social life which the Creator has written into man's moral and spiritual nature. . . . Christians are convinced that the triumphs of the human race are a sign of God's grace and the flowering of His own mysterious design. For the greater man's power becomes, the farther his individual and community responsibility extends. Hence it is clear that men are not deterred by the Christian message from building up the world, or impelled to neglect the welfare of their fellows, but that they are rather more stringently bound to do these very things. (Vatican II, *Gaudium et spes*, 23, 34)

It is appropriate to emphasize the preeminent role that belongs to the laity, both men and women. . . . It is their task to animate temporal realities with Christian commitment, by which they show that they are witnesses and agents of peace and justice. (Pope John Paul II, *Sollicitudo rei socialis*, 47)

1. Why is it important for the church to take a stand on social issues? What can Christian women in particular contribute when they work for justice?

_____

_____

_____

_____

_____

2. What is the relationship between social justice and the proclamation of the gospel? How do we bear witness to Christ through our efforts to promote justice?

_____

_____

_____

_____

_____

3. Why is peace such an important component of justice? How can we actively work against a social evil while still remaining peaceful?

_____

_____

_____

_____

_____

For Further Reflection and Discussion:

1. What have you done in the past or are you doing now to work to promote justice? Do you think you have made a difference?

_____

_____

_____

_____

_____

2. Which social justice issues do you feel most strongly about? Do you think the Lord has put a passion in your heart for those issues? How have you or how can you respond?

_____

_____

_____

_____

_____

3. What qualities of the heart do you think God wants in people who are working for justice? What attitudes may hinder God's work of promoting justice in the world?

_____

_____

_____

_____

_____

4. Share one way in which the social teachings of the church have influenced the way you look at the world. What was it about these teachings that changed or shaped your thinking?

_____

_____

_____

_____

_____

Confidence in Our Call to Share the Good News

16

As Christians, we all want to share the good news—we just don't want to appear pushy, obnoxious, or fanatical! So we tend to keep quiet about our faith, afraid of what other people will think of us or hesitant that we will offend them. However, we are all called to evangelize. We can share the good news of God's love when we ourselves embody that love. If we are attuned to the needs of others, we will be able to reach out with the love of Christ and help them discover the good news for themselves. We can become living witnesses of the difference that God's love has made in our own lives.

Margie was a warm and outgoing person who made it a point to reach out to people, especially to the women in her morning exercise class. She got to know the other women by showing interest in them and by being open and transparent herself. Her faith was the focal point of her life, and she made no effort to hide it. Her prayer time, her Bible study group, the pro-life ministry at her parish—all these topics came up naturally because they were so much a part of her life and who she was. However, Margie never came across as judgmental or self-righteous. Her warm smile made it clear to the other women in her exercise class that she wanted their friendship, even if they did not share her passion for the Lord.

One morning Margie sensed that her friend Josie was feeling low. After class, Margie asked Josie if she wanted to go out for a cup of coffee. At the local diner, Margie asked her if she was okay. Josie burst into tears and poured out her heart about the struggles she was having in her relationship with her husband. Margie listened attentively. Then she offered to pray with Josie, right on the spot. She took Josie's hand and prayed in a quiet voice that God would come into the situation and that Josie would have the grace to let go of her anger and to forgive her husband.

Josie left the diner that morning with a lighter heart, and Margie promised to continue to pray for the relationship. The following week, Margie told Josie she had gone to Mass specifically with the intention of healing for her marriage. Josie knew that God had acted in her life by putting Margie in her class. Even when their exercise class ended, they stayed in touch, and eventually Josie joined Margie's weekly Bible study. Through Margie, Josie met other women of faith who became her friends. She always remained grateful to Margie for reaching out to her with love.

Scripture: John 4:7-26, 28-30, 39, 42

[7]A Samaritan woman came to draw water, and Jesus said to her, "Give me a drink." [8](His disciples had gone to the city to buy food.) [9]The Samaritan woman said to him, "How is it that you, a Jew, ask a drink of me, a woman of Samaria?" (Jews do not share things in common with Samaritans.) [10]Jesus answered her, "If you knew the gift of God, and who it is that is saying to you, 'Give me a drink,' you would have asked him, and he would have given you living water." [11]The woman said to him, "Sir, you have no bucket, and the well is deep. Where do you get that living water? [12]Are you greater than our ancestor Jacob, who gave us the well, and with his sons and his flocks drank from

it?" [13]Jesus said to her, "Everyone who drinks of this water will be thirsty again, [14]but those who drink of the water that I will give them will never be thirsty. The water that I will give will become in them a spring of water gushing up to eternal life." [15]The woman said to him, "Sir, give me this water, so that I may never be thirsty or have to keep coming here to draw water."

[16]Jesus said to her, "Go, call your husband, and come back." [17]The woman answered him, "I have no husband." Jesus said to her, "You are right in saying, 'I have no husband'; [18]for you have had five husbands, and the one you have now is not your husband. What you have said is true!" [19]The woman said to him, "Sir, I see that you are a prophet. [20]Our ancestors worshiped on this mountain, but you say that the place where people must worship is in Jerusalem." [21]Jesus said to her, "Woman, believe me, the hour is coming when you will worship the Father neither on this mountain nor in Jerusalem. [22]You worship what you do not know; we worship what we know, for salvation is from the Jews. [23]But the hour is coming, and is now here, when the true worshipers will worship the Father in spirit and truth, for the Father seeks such as these to worship him. [24]God is spirit, and those who worship him must worship in spirit and truth." [25]The woman said to him, "I know that Messiah is coming" (who is called Christ). "When he comes, he will proclaim all things to us." [26]Jesus said to her, "I am he, the one who is speaking to you." . . .

[28]Then the woman left her water jar and went back to the city. She said to the people, [29]"Come and see a man who told me everything I have ever done! He cannot be the Messiah, can he?" [30]They left the city and were on their way to him. . . .

[39]Many Samaritans from that city believed in him because of the woman's testimony, "He told me everything I have ever done." . . . [42]They said to the woman, "It is no longer because of what you said that we believe, for we have heard for ourselves, and we know that this is truly the Savior of the world."

1. Based on this story, what cues can you take from Jesus about how to evangelize?

_____

_____

_____

_____

_____

2. What made the Samaritan woman so eager to immediately tell others about Jesus? Have you ever felt as compelled as this woman to tell others about Christ? If so, what happened?

_____

_____

_____

_____

_____

3. What invitation did the Samaritan woman offer to her neighbors? How was this effective in bringing others to Jesus?

_____

_____

_____

_____

_____

From the Church:

The laity go forth as powerful proclaimers . . . when they courageously join to their profession of faith a life springing from faith. This evangelization, that is, this announcing of Christ by a living testimony as well as by the spoken word, takes on a specific quality and a special force in that it is carried out in the ordinary surroundings of the world. (*Lumen gentium*, 35)

There are innumerable opportunities open to the laity for the exercise of their apostolate of evangelization and sanctification. The very testimony of their Christian life and good works done in a supernatural spirit have the power to draw men to belief and to God. . . . However, an apostolate of this kind does not consist only in the witness of one's way of life; a true apostle looks for opportunities to announce Christ by words addressed either to non-believers with a view to leading them to faith, or to the faithful with a view to instructing, strengthening, and encouraging them to a more fervent life. (Pope Paul VI, *Apostolicam actositatem*, Decree on the Apostolate of the Laity, 6)

1. Why should we have confidence that God is calling us to evangelize the world? How does viewing evangelization as a call from God change the way we approach it?

_____

_____

_____

_____

_____

2. How do you proclaim Christ by the way you live? How can you imitate the Samaritan woman in telling others about your own encounter with Jesus?

_____

_____

_____

_____

_____

3. Who among your acquaintances may not have an opportunity to hear the good news if you don't tell them yourself? How can you introduce the topic without putting them on the defensive?

_____

_____

_____

_____

_____

For Further Reflection and Discussion:

1. Share your personal story of how the Lord has changed your life. In what ways might writing down your own faith journey prepare you to become a more effective witness?

_____

_____

_____

_____

_____

2. What might be preventing you from sharing the good news more often or with more people? What can you do to overcome these obstacles? What, if any, obstacles have you encountered in talking with family members about your faith?

_____

_____

_____

_____

_____

3. How often do you talk to the young people in your life about your faith? How will sharing how God has worked in your life, even in everyday experiences, help your children or other family members to recognize God in their own lives?

_____

_____

_____

_____

_____

4. Ask the Holy Spirit to bring to your mind one person who is open to hearing the good news. Perhaps you could invite him or her to come to Mass with you or to lunch or dinner. You may just want to drop a note telling that person you are praying for them.

_____

_____

_____

_____

_____

Also From The Word Among Us Press

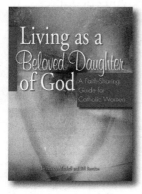

**Living as a Beloved Daughter of God:
A Faith-Sharing Guide for
Catholic Women**

Patricia Mitchell and Bill Bawden

How many Catholic women think of themselves first and foremost as beloved daughters of God? This sixteen-session faith-sharing guide will help women come to a deeper understanding of their identity in Christ while also helping them to gain a renewed perspective of their varied roles as wives, mothers, sisters, and daughters.

112 pages, 5¾ x 8⅜, softcover.

Item# BGSTE4